...AMAZING... MAGIC ...TRICKS!...

BY NORM BARNHART

raintree
a Capstone company—publishers for children
www.raintree.co.uk

Raintree is an imprint of Capstone Global Library Limited, a company incorporated in England and Wales having its registered office at 264 Banbury Road, Oxford, OX2 7DY – Registered company number: 6695582
www.raintree.co.uk
myorders@raintree.co.uk

Edited by Aaron Sautter
Designed by Ted Williams and Elyse
Picture research by Eric Gohl
Production by Katy LaVigne
Printed and bound in India.

ISBN 978 1 4747 5531 3
23 22 21 20 19
10 9 8 7 6 5 4 3 2 1

British Library Cataloguing in Publication Data
A full catalogue record for this book is available from the British Library.

Image Credits
All photographs and video are done by Capstone Studio

Design Elements
Shutterstock: findracadabra, G.roman, javarman, popular business

Every effort has been made to contact copyright holders of material reproduced in this book. Any omissions will be rectified in subsequent printings if notice is given to the publisher.

All the internet addresses (URLs) given in this book were valid at the time of going to press. However, due to the dynamic nature of the internet, some addresses may have changed, or sites may have changed or ceased to exist since publication. While the author and publisher regret any inconvenience this may cause readers, no responsibility for any such changes can be accepted by either the author or the publisher

CONTENTS

WELCOME TO THE WORLD OF
MAGIC

If you've ever wanted to astound people with your mystical magical abilities, you've picked up the right book! You don't need to be a master magician to perform amazing magic. With this book you can learn many simple, fun tricks that will be sure to astonish an audience. Whether you're performing for a few friends or a large crowd, you'll be dazzling audiences with fantastic magic in no time!

MEET THE MAGICIAN!

Norm Barnhart is a professional comic magician who has entertained audiences for nearly 40 years. In 2007, Norm was named America's Funniest Magician by the Family Entertainers Workshop. Norm's travels have taken him across the United States and to many countries around the world. Norm says, **"I love to bring smiles to people of all ages with magic. After reading this book, kids will love performing magic tricks for their friends too."**

THE KEYS TO MAGIC

⭐ **Practise, practise, practise!** Try standing in front of a mirror while practising with your props. Then you can see what the tricks look like to your audience.

⭐ **Keep it secret!** If you reveal the secrets of a trick, people won't be very impressed. It also ruins the trick for other magicians.

⭐ **Be entertaining!** Tell the audience jokes or stories while you do your tricks. It will keep them coming back for more.

BEFORE YOU BEGIN

Most magicians hide their props in a magic box. A magic box will help you keep your tricks organized and your special props hidden from the audience. You can use a box found at a craft shop. Or you can make your own magic box. Find a cardboard box and decorate it with some colourful stars, or cover it with dark cloth so it looks mysterious.

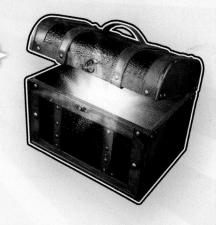

A magic wand is one of a magician's most useful tools. Wands help direct people's attention to what you want them to see. You can make a wand out of a wooden dowel painted black and white. Or roll up a piece of black construction paper and tape the ends. You can add sparkles and stars if you wish. Be creative and have fun!

THE MAGICAL SAILOR'S KNOT

Magicians need fast hands. In this trick, you'll make a knot instantly appear on a rope. Your friends will be amazed at your incredible hand speed!

WHAT YOU NEED

✪ a piece of rope about 60 centimetres (2 feet) long

PREPARATION

1. Tie a large knot in one end of the rope as shown.

PERFORMANCE

1. First, show the audience the rope. Hold it with the knot secretly hidden in your hand as shown.

MAGIC TIP

By failing at first, the audience will be more amazed when you make the knot seem to magically appear.

6

2. Now, hold the other end of the rope between your thumb and first finger. Make sure you keep the knot hidden. Tell the audience that your hands are faster than the eye, and that you can make a knot appear out of thin air.

3. With your free hand, pretend to grab an invisible knot out of the air. Then throw it at the rope.

As you throw the invisible knot, let go of the untied end. Say, "Oops, I missed. I'll try again."

4. Hold the untied end up like before. Pretend to throw the invisible knot again and drop the untied end. Say, "Oh, I missed again." Act a bit disappointed and then try a third time.

The third time it will work. This time let go of the end with the knot. The knot magically appears on the rope!

THE MAGIC ROBOT

These robots seem to have magical abilities! In this trick, the audience will gasp when they see a toy robot magically transport from your pocket back to its box.

PREPARATION

1. First, cut a hole in the side of the box as shown. The hole should only be large enough to fit your finger. Then place both robots into the box.

PERFORMANCE

1. Start by picking up the box with one finger inside the hole. Hold one toy robot with your finger as shown. Next, tip over the box to drop the second robot into your open hand. Make sure you tip the box towards yourself so the audience won't see the secret robot inside.

2. Next, hold up the robot and show it to the audience. Tell them a story about how it can perform an amazing magic act. Explain how it can move so fast that they won't even see it move. Then place the robot in your pocket.

3. Hold up the box and wave your magic wand over it. You can say some made-up magic words to help fool the audience. Or you can pretend that you feel something jump out of your pocket and into the box.

4. Finally tip over the box to drop the secret robot into your hand. Show it to the audience and make it take a bow!

MAGIC TIP Make sure you keep the hole in the box hidden at all times. If the audience sees it, they'll learn the secret of the trick.

THE ZOOMING MOON ROCK

Even rocks can get homesick. Here's a trick you can use to send a lonely Moon rock zooming back home to the Moon. Everybody will be left wondering how it's done!

WHAT YOU NEED

- ⭐ s small, shiny rock
- ⭐ two foam cups
- ⭐ scissors

PREPARATION

1. First, make a secret hole by cutting out the bottom of one foam cup with the scissors as shown.

2. Next, stack the cups so the cup with the secret hole is on the bottom. Then put the rock in the top cup as shown.

1. First, ask a volunteer in the audience to help you with this trick. Put the Moon rock into the volunteer's hand and ask him or her to show it to the audience. Then tell the audience a story about magical Moon rocks that fly home to the Moon when they get lonely.

2. Now, separate the cups. Make sure you hide the secret hole by keeping that cup in the palm of your hand as shown. Tell the audience that you're going to send the rock home with some help from your volunteer. Then get the volunteer to put the rock back in the normal cup.

Secret hole

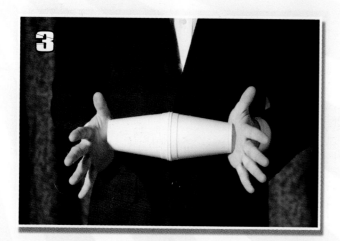

3. Next, place the two cups together top to top as shown.

4. Tip over the cups so the rock falls through the secret hole and into your hand. Make sure you keep the hole covered with your hand so the audience can't see it.

Hidden rock

5. Next, set the cups on the table so they are stacked top to top as shown. Make sure you keep the rock hidden in your hand.

6. Now, reach into your magic box with the hand holding the rock. Ditch the rock in the box and grab your magic wand.

7. Here's where the magic happens! Wave your magic wand over the stacked cups. You can ask your volunteer to repeat some magic words to help send the rock home too. Then pretend to watch the rock zoom home to the moon.

8. Finally, slam your hand down on the stacked cups to smash them up. Tear up the pieces to show that the rock has disappeared into outer space! Thank the volunteer and ask your audience to give him or her a round of applause!

MAGIC TIP Try asking the volunteer to wave the magic wand over the cups. He or she will be astounded that the rock disappeared!

THE TRICKY LIZARD

Most reptiles aren't very fast. But this tricky lizard can zip out of sight in a split second. Your audience will have a good laugh when they see it climbing on your back!

WHAT YOU NEED

⭐ a poster or book showing the desert
⭐ a small toy lizard
⭐ black thread
⭐ a safety pin
⭐ a black jacket

PREPARATION

1. First, tie one end of the thread to the safety pin and the other end to the toy lizard. Then attach the pin to the back of your shirt or jacket collar as shown.

Pin

2. Next, bring the toy lizard under your arm so the thread runs under it as shown. Then place the lizard in your breast pocket. The audience should not be able to see the thread when it's hidden against the black jacket.

Thread

1. Pull the toy lizard out of your pocket and show it to the audience. Tell them a story about how hard it is to keep track of the tricky reptile. Let them know it often disappears and tries to get back to its desert home.

2. Next, cover the lizard with the desert picture. As you do this, secretly drop the lizard and let it swing around to land on your back. Then pull away the picture to show that the lizard has vanished!

3. Now, pretend to look around for the tricky lizard. Where did it go? Ask the audience if they saw where it went. Finally, turn around. The audience will see the lizard hanging on your back. Act amazed and confused about how it got there. The audience will get a big laugh out of this trick!

FIND THE MAGIC RABBIT

Lots of magicians like pulling rabbits out of their hats. But there's more than one way to find a magic rabbit. In this trick, a magical paper bunny is the star of the show!

WHAT YOU NEED

- ⭐ a felt-tip pen or crayon
- ⭐ a sheet of paper
- ⭐ a colourful handkerchief

PREPARATION

1. Draw a carrot, a bunny and a hat on the paper as shown. Make sure the bunny is in the centre. Leave plenty of space between each picture.

PERFORMANCE

1. First, show the audience the paper with the three pictures. Then fold the paper between the pictures and tear it into three pieces along the folds.

16

2. Next, turn the pictures over. Ask a volunteer to mix the pictures up and cover them with the hanky while your back is turned.

3. When the volunteer has finished, turn back to the table. With a mysterious look on your face say, "I can find the bunny without looking under the hanky." Then reach under the hanky to get the rabbit.

Torn sides

4. Now, pull out the picture of the rabbit and take a bow! The secret to this trick is easy. When you reach under the hanky, simply feel the sides of each piece of paper. As the rabbit is drawn on the centre piece, it is the only paper with two torn sides. It's a simple trick that will keep your friends guessing how it's done!

MAGIC TIP Try this trick with some different drawings. You could draw the faces of two boys and a girl, or two dogs and a cat.

THE FREAKY MIND WELD

Paper clips are easy to lose. It's easier to keep track of them if they're linked together. This trick will astonish your audience when they see your magic mental powers at work!

WHAT YOU NEED
- ★ 20 paper clips
- ★ an envelope
- ★ glue

PREPARATION

1. First, link together 10 paper clips and place them in the corner of the envelope. Next, glue the inside of the envelope as shown to make a secret pocket. The linked clips will be sealed inside. Then put the 10 loose clips into the open part of the envelope.

Glue here.

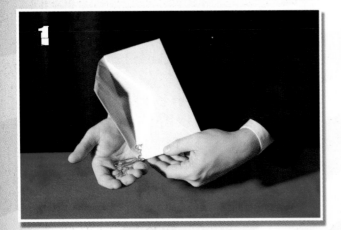

PERFORMANCE

1. Show the envelope to the audience and say, "I've found an easy way to keep paper clips together." Open the envelope and pour out the loose clips.

MAGIC TIP

Try attaching a small toy soldier to the end of the paper clip chain. Then pretend to be surprised when you find that the soldier did all the work!

2. Tell the audience, "All I have to do is link the clips together with my mind." Put the clips back in the envelope, one at a time. Count out loud as you do this so the audience knows how many paper clips there are. Then lick the envelope and seal it.

3. Now, hold the envelope up to your forehead. Pretend to use your powerful mental energy to link the paper clips together. Pretending to concentrate hard makes this trick seem really mysterious for the audience.

4. Now, rip open the end of the envelope with the secret pocket. Grab the end of the linked clips and slowly pull them out. The audience will be astonished when they see that the clips are linked together. You have one powerful brain!

THE CRAZY COMICAL SOCK

The best way to warm up an audience is to get them laughing. With this trick, the audience gets a good laugh when you find something you didn't even know was lost!

WHAT YOU NEED

⚙ two identical socks   ⚙ a black hat

⚙ a piece of black cloth   ⚙ four safety pins

PREPARATION

1. First, pin or sew the black cloth into the bottom of the hat to create a secret pocket as shown. Then tuck a sock into the pocket.

2. Next, put the other sock on one foot. Leave your other foot bare inside your shoe as shown.

20

1. Start by telling the audience that you often find strange things in your hat. Tell them, "I never know what I might get when I do this trick." Then hold the hat up to show the audience that it's empty.

2. Now, wave your magic wand over the hat and say a few mysterious magic words.

3. Reach into the hat and pull out the sock. Make a funny, confused look. The audience will think something has gone wrong.

4. While looking confused, lift up your trouser leg to show the matching sock that you're wearing. Then quickly lift your other trouser leg to show that the sock is missing. Act surprised or embarrassed — as if you made the sock appear in the hat by mistake. The audience will have a good laugh!

THE SPOOKY SPOON

Even ghosts like to go on picnics. Your friends will be spooked when this ghostly spoon disappears right before their eyes! With practice, you can make this simple trick look amazing!

WHAT YOU NEED

- ★ a plastic spoon
- ★ about 60 centimetres (2 feet) of thin elastic cord
- ★ a safety pin
- ★ a jacket with long sleeves
- ★ an electric drill

PREPARATION

1. First, ask an adult to drill a small hole in the end of the spoon handle as shown. Then tie one end of the elastic thread through the hole in the spoon and the other end to the safety pin.

2. Next, connect the safety pin to the inside of your jacket at the collar. Then run the spoon and elastic down the inside of the jacket sleeve as shown.

1. Just before you do this trick, step off the stage or behind the curtain so the audience can't see you. Pull the spoon out of your sleeve and hold it in your hand as shown. Tell the audience a spooky story about the ghostly spoon. Say, "This spoon belongs to a ghost. Sometimes it takes the spoon back without any warning!"

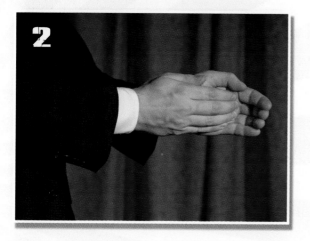

2. Now, pretend to try and grab the spoon with both hands. As you do this, let go of the spoon.

3. When you let go of the spoon, let it slide back up your sleeve as shown.

4. Finally, open your hands and show the audience that the spoon has vanished into thin air. Say, "Looks like the ghost was ready for his dinner and wanted his spoon back!"

INVISIBLE MAGIC GLUE

Your friends will wonder how your wand sticks to your hand with this mysterious trick. They'll be amazed when the wand falls off with a snap of their fingers!

PERFORMANCE

1. Any small bottle will work for this trick. Start by telling your audience that the bottle holds invisible magic glue.

Next, hold your wand in one hand and pretend to pour the glue all over the wand and your hand.

2. Close your hand around the wand and put the bottle back in your magic box.

Now, grip your wrist with your other hand. Slide your finger up to hold the wand as shown, hiding it behind your open hand. Keep your wand and finger facing away from the audience. If your friends see your finger, the trick will be ruined!

24

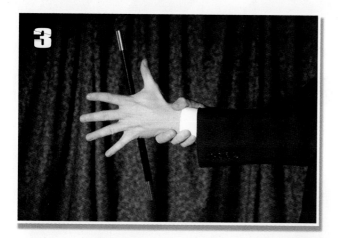

3. Next, slowly open your hand to show that the wand is stuck in place. Say, "This invisible glue is some really sticky stuff!"

4. When you want the glue to disappear, just ask a friend to snap his or her fingers. At that moment, let the wand go by moving your finger. The wand is no longer stuck to your hand!

MAGIC TIP Try using your acting skills to add humour to this trick. Pretend that the wand won't come off, no matter how hard you shake your hand!

THE PHOENIX BALLOON

Is it possible to put a popped balloon back together again? It is with this fun trick! The audience will be stunned when they see a popped balloon magically made whole again.

WHAT YOU NEED

⭐ two identical balloons
⭐ a large paper bag
⭐ a fork

PREPARATION

1. First, blow up one balloon and tie it. Then place it at the bottom of the paper bag as shown. Place the empty balloon in the bag so it can be tipped out easily.

PERFORMANCE

1. Start by telling the audience about your magic balloon. Say, "This balloon can restore itself if it's popped!" Then tip over the bag so the empty balloon drops onto the table. Don't let the secret blown-up balloon fall out.

MAGIC TIP

Try adding some fun to this trick. Pretend that the balloon pieces are jumping around in the bag as they try to join together again.

2. Next, blow up the empty balloon, tie it and show it to the audience. Then pop it with the fork and place the pieces back into the bag. You can have fun by saying something like, "This looks bad. I don't know if the balloon can fix itself this time!"

3. Now, close the top of the bag and wave your magic wand over it. You can say a few made-up magic words too.

4. Finally, open up the bag and pull out the secret blown-up balloon. The audience will think the popped balloon has magically restored itself. Take a bow as they applaud!

TOMMY, THE TRAINED PING-PONG BALL

Normal ping-pong balls just bounce around a lot. But this magic ping-pong ball can do a great trick. People will be astonished when it does an amazing balancing act!

WHAT YOU NEED

- ⭐ a ping-pong ball
- ⭐ a magic wand
- ⭐ black thread
- ⭐ tape
- ⭐ scissors
- ⭐ a table

PREPARATION

1. First, cut a piece of thread a bit longer than the magic wand. Then use small pieces of tape to attach the thread to the wand on both ends. Make sure the thread stays a bit loose in the middle.

PERFORMANCE

1. Start by bouncing the ping-pong ball on the table a couple of times. Tell the audience a story about the ball. Say, "Tommy looks like a normal ping-pong ball. But he is really a magic ball. He can do a fun balancing act!"

28

2. When you're ready to do the trick, hold the wand with your thumbs under the thread as shown. The thread will help balance the ball.

3. Make sure you keep the thread facing you so the audience can't see it. Now, place the ball on the wand and balance it on the thread.

4. To the audience, the ball will look as if it is balancing on the wand. Gently tilt the wand up and down a bit so the ball travels back and forth. The ball will seem to be doing a dangerous balancing act.

To end the trick, throw the ball up in the air, catch it and throw it to someone in the audience. While they look at it, throw the wand into your magic box. Then ask the audience for a round of applause for Tommy, the tricky ping-pong ball!

THE MAGIC HANKY

Some people carry hankies in case they have to sneeze. Where do you think magicians keep their hankies? With this fun trick, you can make a colourful hanky appear from an empty paper bag!

WHAT YOU NEED

- ★ two small paper bags
- ★ scissors
- ★ a colourful handkerchief
- ★ colourful confetti

PREPARATION

1. For this trick, you'll need a secret pocket in the bottom of a paper bag. To make it, cut the top half off of one paper bag. Keep the bottom half for the next step.

2. Next, place the hanky at the bottom of the second bag. Then place the half bag inside the whole bag on top of the hanky. The hanky is now hidden inside the secret pocket. Now it's time to trick the audience!

1. First, tell the audience about your magic confetti that can create a new hanky any time you need one. Next, pick up the bag and show the audience that it's empty by turning it upside down. Ask a volunteer to stick a hand in the bag to make sure it's empty.

2. Now, throw some of the colourful confetti into the bag. Wave your wand over the bag and say a few magic words.

Next, blow the bag up like a balloon. Then twist the top and pop the bag so the confetti flies out as shown.

3. After startling the audience with the loud bang, it's time to amaze them by pulling out the colourful hanky. Say something like, "This magic confetti is great. It works every time!"

MAGIC TIP

If you have a rainbow-coloured hanky, ask the audience to pretend to take a tiny pinch of colour off their tops and flick it towards the bag. Then a rainbow-coloured hanky amazingly appears!

THE MAGIC MATCHBOX BANK

You can save money without making a trip to the bank! Just sprinkle some magic dust and your coins travel to a safe place. This magical travelling penny will keep your audience in awe.

WHAT YOU NEED

⭐ two pennies
⭐ an empty matchbox

PREPARATION

1. Place one of the pennies between the inner and outer parts of the matchbox as shown. Make sure the penny is completely covered so the audience won't see it.

PERFORMANCE

1. First, show the audience that the matchbox is empty. Say, "I've found a new kind of savings bank." Then close the box so the secret penny slides into it and set it aside. Next, take out the second penny and show it to the audience.

Hidden penny

2. Now, hold the penny between your thumb and first finger. Then pretend to grab the penny with your other hand. But instead of grabbing it, you will drop it into your palm as shown. It looks like you're holding the coin in the second hand, but you are really hiding it in the palm of the first hand. This old trick is called the French Drop. Practise this move until it looks smooth and natural.

3. Now, reach into your pocket for some invisible magic dust with the hand holding the penny. Leave the penny in your pocket, then pretend to sprinkle magic dust over your empty hand.

4. Next, open your hands wide to show the audience that the penny has vanished!

5. Finally, open the matchbox and take out the secret penny. Show it to the audience. They will be stunned that the penny has magically travelled from your hand to the matchbox!

MESSAGE FROM A GHOST

You can freak out your friends with this spooky trick. When your pet ghost sends you a creepy message, they'll be too scared to move!

PREPARATION

1. Write a creepy message like "Boo!" on one sheet of paper. Crumple the message into a ball. Then place it into the shoebox with the blank sheet of paper. Place the pen in your pocket.

Message

PERFORMANCE

1. Tell your friends you have a pet ghost and that it likes to leave you messages. Get out the shoebox and take out the blank sheet of paper. At the same time, secretly hide the crumpled secret message in your hand as shown.

MAGIC TIP

Before doing this trick, try telling the audience a story about the ghost. Maybe you trapped it by the light of the full moon. Or maybe it's a friendly ghost that likes to help out with your magic show!

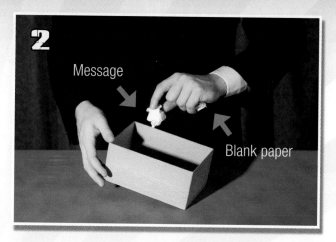

Message

Blank paper

2. Show the audience that the flat paper is blank on both sides, then crumple it into a ball. As you crumple it, carefully swap it with the secret message hidden in your hand. Then drop the secret message into the shoebox. Keep the crumpled blank paper hidden in your hand.

3. Next, get the pen from your pocket. As you do this, leave the crumpled blank paper behind in your pocket. Put the pen into the box and then put the lid on. Begin shaking the box and pretending to wrestle with it as if your pet ghost is moving around inside.

4. Finally, remove the shoebox lid and take out the paper with the secret message. Ask someone to open it and read it. Your friends will be amazed at the spooky message that has appeared!

THE MYSTERIOUS CAR TRICK

You can use the power of your mind to find a shiny, cool car hidden in a paper bag. Your incredible mental powers will baffle people with this trick!

WHAT YOU NEED

- a pencil
- three small paper bags
- one shiny toy car
- two dull toy cars

PREPARATION

1. Place a small, secret pencil mark in the bottom corner of one bag as shown. Don't make the mark too dark, or someone might see it and learn how this trick works.

Secret mark

PERFORMANCE

1. First, show the three cars to the audience. Place the shiny cool car in the marked bag. Place the dull cars in the other bags. Then fold over the tops of all three bags. Keep the secret mark facing you so nobody sees it.

MAGIC TIP

Try acting as if you don't know which bag is correct at first. Ask the volunteer to help by mixing up the bags even more. The audience will be astonished when you find the cool car!

2. Tell the audience about your amazing mental powers. Say, "I can use my mind to find the cool car even if the bags are mixed up." Then turn around and ask a volunteer from the audience to mix up the bags.

3. Now, turn back to the table and pretend to use your mental powers to find the cool car. Hold up each bag and look at it closely. Pretend to concentrate hard on what's inside. While doing this, you will really be looking for the bag with the secret mark.

4. When you find the marked bag say, "This is it! I've found the cool car." Reach in and pull out the cool car. Take a bow as the audience applauds your amazing mental powers!

MULTIPLYING MONEY

Everybody likes having plenty of money. Magic with money really grabs people's attention. This trick will make the audience wish their money could multiply this fast!

PREPARATION

1. First, create a secret pocket by taping the craft sticks to the bottom of the table as shown. The space between them should be a bit smaller than the coins are wide. Make sure the pocket is near the side of the table you'll be sitting at.

2. Next, slide two coins into the secret pocket. The gap between the sticks should allow you to easily get at the coins.

1. Start by laying out five coins on the table. Tell your audience, "Making money is easy. I can make these coins multiply." Ask a volunteer to count the coins on the table.

2. Now, slide the coins off the edge of the table with one hand so they drop into your other hand.

3. At the same time, use your second hand to slide the coins out of the secret pocket as shown.

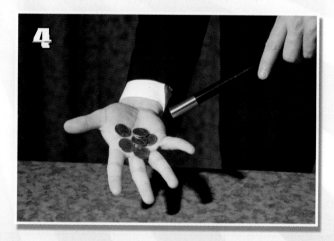

4. Close your hand around the coins. Then pretend to grab some invisible coins from the air and throw them into your hand. Wave your magic wand over your hand in a mystical way and say a few magic words. Finally, open your hand and ask the volunteer to recount the coins. The audience will be stunned when they see that the coins have multiplied!

THE AMAZING BRAIN-E-O

Use the power of your brain to read people's minds! Your friends will be amazed as you tell them what objects they are thinking about. It's easy when you know the secret.

WHAT YOU NEED

* ten random objects
* a secret assistant

PERFORMANCE

1. Start this trick by talking about your amazing mind-reading powers. Tell the audience that you can read their minds – and you can prove it. Ask your secret assistant to sit with the audience. When you perform this trick, ask him or her to come up and help you.

2. Then turn your back to the audience. While your back is turned, your assistant asks someone in the audience to choose a prop on the table. The volunteer should not say the object's name out loud. Instead, the volunteer should just point at the chosen object.

MAGIC TIP

Try this trick a second time, but next time the chosen prop will be the sixth one the assistant points to. The audience will wonder how you can read their minds!

3. Before doing this trick, you should arrange for your assistant to point at the chosen prop on the third try. Now, turn back to the table. Your assistant should point to a different object and ask if it is the chosen item. You'll say, "No, that's not correct."

4. Your assistant then points to a second item on the table. Concentrate hard on that object and act as if you aren't sure if it's correct. Finally, you'll say, "No that's not the right one either."

5. On the third try, your assistant will point at the correct object. Now, act as if the trick has become really easy and say, "Yes, that's it!" The audience will be stunned by your amazing mind-reading powers!

THE CONFUSING COIN MYSTERY

Sometimes coins are found in the strangest places. This trick will stun your audience when extra coins magically appear in a volunteer's hands.

WHAT YOU NEED

✪ eight coins
✪ an old book
✪ scissors
✪ glue

PREPARATION

1. First, make a secret pocket in the old book. Cut out a small space at the bottom of the book as shown. Make sure the pocket is big enough to fit two coins inside. Don't make it too big or the audience might see the hole.

2. To help keep the pages together, glue them around the secret pocket as shown. When the glue is dry, place two coins in the secret pocket.

MAGIC TIP

Always keep the secret pocket facing you so the audience and volunteer can't see the hole with the hidden coins.

1. Tell the audience a story about finding magical invisible coins in the air. Then place six coins on top of the book. Ask a volunteer to count the coins out loud with you. Then ask the volunteer to hold out his or her hands. Quickly tip the book so all the coins, including the hidden ones, slide into the volunteer's hands.

2. Tell the volunteer to hold the coins tightly. Then pretend to find two invisible coins in the air. Pretend to throw the coins through the book into the volunteer's hand. Ask, "Did you feel anything happen inside your hand?" The volunteer will probably say they didn't feel anything at all.

3. Finally, ask the volunteer to put the coins on the table and count them out loud again. The audience will be amazed when they see there are now eight coins. Thank the volunteer and ask the audience to give him or her a round of applause!

THE AMAZING APPEARING BALL

"Where did that ball come from?" That's what your friends will say when you make this ball magically appear from an empty cup!

WHAT YOU NEED

- ⭐ a ping-pong ball
- ⭐ a foam cup
- ⭐ a magic wand

PREPARATION

1. First, make a hole in the foam cup so your finger can poke into it.

Now, place the ball in the cup and use your third finger to hold it in place as shown.

MAGIC TIP

Add some fun to this trick by drawing a face on the ball and giving it a fun name. Pretend that it likes to play hide-and-seek!

1. First, tip over the cup to show that it's empty. Then tell the audience, "Things aren't always as they appear. This cup might look empty, but it's not." Make sure you don't let anyone see the ball or your finger inside the cup!

2. Now, hold the cup up high and wave your magic wand over it. While you do this, you can say a few made-up magic words.

3. Finally, tip over the cup and let the ball fall into your open hand. The ball magically appears!

Show the audience the ball and throw it to someone. While they're looking at the ball, throw the special cup into your magic box. Nobody will ever know the secret!

THE MYSTIC SNOWFLAKE

No two snowflakes are exactly alike. With this trick you can make a paper snowflake with special magical scissors. The audience won't believe their eyes when it magically appears!

WHAT YOU NEED

⭐ two sheets of paper
⭐ scissors

PREPARATION

1. First, fold one sheet of paper in half three or four times. Then cut a few pieces out around the edges to make a paper snowflake.

Hidden snowflake

PERFORMANCE

1. Leave the paper snowflake folded up. When you're ready to do the trick, take the plain paper out of your magic box. At the same time, hide the paper snowflake in your hand as shown.

2. Tell the audience you can make a snowflake with magic invisible scissors. Show them the plain paper and fold it three or four times. With the final fold, secretly swap the plain paper with the snowflake. Hide the plain paper in the palm of your hand. Make sure the audience doesn't see you swap the two pieces of paper.

Snowflake

Hidden paper

3. Next, use the hand that is hiding the plain paper to reach into your pocket for your magic invisible scissors. Leave the paper behind in your pocket.

4. Now, pretend to pull out the magic invisible scissors. Use your fingers like scissors as shown, and pretend to cut out a paper snowflake.

5. Finally, unfold the paper snowflake and show it to the audience. They'll be amazed when they see that the paper has been transformed right before their eyes!

SPECIAL MAGICAL SECRETS

PALMING

Magicians often use a method called palming to make things seem to vanish into thin air. To do it, they secretly hide an object in the palm of their hand. Try practising palming in front of a mirror so your hand looks natural. Once you learn to palm objects, you'll be able to astonish your friends!

SECRET ASSISTANTS

Magicians often have secret assistants who know how the tricks work. Sometimes they sit in the crowd and pretend to be part of the audience. Secret assistants help the magician make the tricks look real. Find a good secret assistant and you'll have lots of fun fooling people with your magic tricks.

THE DITCH

The Ditch, or secret drop, is one of the most valuable secrets in magic. As you grab your magic wand out of your magic box, you secretly drop a hidden object into the box. Don't look stiff or nervous while you do this. Just be calm while you smoothly make the switch. The audience won't suspect a thing!

MISDIRECTION

Misdirection is an important part of magic. Magicians misdirect audiences by focusing their eyes on what they want people to look at. Then they can secretly hide an object in their pocket or magic box while the audience is focused on something else. With practice, you can be a master of misdirection too!